CHINATOWN GHOSTS

CHINATOWN GHOSTS

The Poems and Photographs of
Jim Wong-Chu

ARSENAL PULP PRESS
VANCOUVER

ARSENAL PULP PRESS
Suite 202 – 211 East Georgia St.
Vancouver, BC V6A 1Z6
Canada
arsenalpulp.com

The publisher gratefully acknowledges the support of the Canada Council for the Arts and the British Columbia Arts Council for its publishing program, and the Government of Canada, and the Government of British Columbia (through the Book Publishing Tax Credit Program), for its publishing activities.

Arsenal Pulp Press acknowledges the xʷməθkʷəy̓əm (Musqueam), Sḵwx̱wú7mesh (Squamish), and səlilwətaʔɬ (Tsleil-Waututh) Nations, speakers of Hul'q'umi'num'/Halq'eméylem/hən̓q̓əmin̓əm̓ and custodians of the traditional, ancestral, and unceded territories where our office is located. We pay respect to their histories, traditions, and continuous living cultures and commit to accountability, respectful relations, and friendship.

Some of these poems appeared in *West Coast Review, Asianadian, Mainstream,* and *Potlatch,* as well as *Inalienable Rice: A Chinese and Japanese Canadian Anthology* (Powell Street Revue and the Chinese Canadian Writers' Workshop, 1979), and *Gold Mountain: The Chinese in the New World,* Anthony B. Chan (New Star, 1983).

Lines quoted from *Year of the Dragon* are taken from *Two Plays by Frank Chin* (University of Washington Press, 1981).

Cover and text design by Oliver McPartlin

Printed and bound in Canada

Library and Archives Canada Cataloguing in Publication:

Wong-Chu, Jim, 1949-, author
　　　Chinatown ghosts : the poems and photographs of Jim Wong-Chu.
— 2nd edition.
Issued in print and electronic formats.
ISBN 978-1-55152-748-2 (softcover).--ISBN 978-1-55152-749-9 (HTML)
　　　I. Title.
PS8595.O598C5 2018　　　　　　C811'.54　　　　　C2018-903422-X
　　　　　　　　　　　　　　　　　　　　　　　　　　C2018-903423-8

This book is dedicated
to the memory of
Garrick Chu

Special thanks to Alvin Jang, J. Michael Yates, Paul Yee,
SKY Lee, Helen Koyama, Jane Munro, George McWhirter,
Flo, Sid, and Marlene who believed in me.

Contents

A Chinatown Ghost:
In Loving Memory of Jim Wong-Chu

I remember the long drives home after our meetings.
Jim liked choreographing the main points, teaching me how to read between the lines, meticulously setting the stage for his next big idea for the Asian Canadian Writers' Workshop. One time, just as he was about to drop me off, he told me to shut the door and continued talking, and half an hour later, with the engine still running, he changed the way I thought about writing.

"Canada is a very unique place because you can do whatever you want, but you just have to do it yourself," Jim was apt to say. "*No one else is going to do it for you.*" So that's what Jim Wong-Chu did. When he got tired of photography, he picked up the pen and became a poet, and later, when knew he could do more by helping others, he dropped his pen to become an editor, and then director of a festival that he founded to celebrate Asian Canadian writing.

Jim has been called a pioneer numerous times, even described in *BC Bookworld* as the "Moses of Asian Canadian literature," but Jim's displaced youth meant that he never completed his formal education. He never hid this fact. It only fuelled his curiosity for learning. He was tireless, often sleeping only a few hours and rising at four a.m. to type an email to finish off a thought and get ready for another project he was working on.

Jim's success was his determination: he liked having the last word, to script the narrative his way. His persistence in consistency meant writers—both known and unknown, nobodies and somebodies—knew him simply as the person to go to for advice about writing. He never turned away anyone who had a story to tell, regardless of how unready it might have been.

Jim lived a simple life that breathed Asian Canadian literature. "I'm not better than anyone else, I've just done it for a long time," he once told me, and because of this longevity in the literary world, he probably came across, talked to, and read the manuscripts of a whole generation of Asian Canadian writers. His archives at the University of British Columbia tell the story.

Jim led the Asian Canadian Writers' Workshop from the beginning, before it even had a name. He loved his life outside of work, probably working harder than anyone who gets paid at their own job. "You can never give me enough for what I do," Jim quipped once, and it was true: he never got paid a penny for the hours he put into his beloved ACWW, *Ricepaper Magazine,* and LiterASIAN festival.

It's very difficult to live up to Jim's expectations. His legacy consists of some of the finest writers in the country. When he wanted to take the ACWW to the next level and be serious about supporting writers, he rolled up his sleeves. He wanted to learn the role of publisher, so he went to Arsenal Pulp Press after his day was done at Canada Post and honed his craft by watching and observing. He wanted to be able to speak the nuanced language of literary agents while understanding the trials of fledgling writers.

If there was any Midas to his touch, it was the ability to instill confidence in his ideas, to convince with remarkable resolution. People couldn't understand Jim's attachment to *Ricepaper Magazine*. But it was his plot line: a way to write his stories through the imaginations of young and emerging Asian Canadians writers. He often gave them tidbits and stories to begin with, and along the way he nurtured a generation of writers, who continue to write the literary map of Canada.

Jim liked telling the story of a fortune teller in Hong Kong who told him that he would be very rich but would die very young. So Jim took the soothsayer's prophecy to heart. Shooting the breeze with people mattered more to him than all the money in the world.

Jim's gift to me was his wisdom. He urged me to type out the passages of my favourite authors, to simulate how writers processed language. He instructed me to read the stories of O. Henry, to learn how to properly tell a story. He told me to stand on a chair and drop index cards with words on the floor to see the patterns of verse. Jim's eclectic ways of tutelage were a mastering of his literary disciples.

Jim's influence continues. Reading his poems again, I feel his spirit hovering above, nodding. He was proud of *Chinatown Ghosts* and went to the library to sign it out to keep it in circulation, to remain relevant, so that his words would continue to be shared for yet another day.

I'll miss those long drives home, Jim. Thank you for the lift.

ALLAN CHO

Early on a spring morning, I sat in the only parked car on Pender Street in Chinatown.

The vehicle had an important way of making me invisible in person. In effect, I was not me but a Corolla, back in the day when the first ones brought into Canada were almost all the same stolid tone of orange.

I had gotten there just after daybreak to set up. The place was totally deserted, except for the clanking of garbage pickup in the alley. Hey, I must have been determined, because at that time of life sleep was for me a very difficult thing to forfeit. It would be decades before I learned that the brain reaches full maturity at around twenty-three to twenty-five years of age. I was a bit shy of that and a sickly sort to boot.

Nonetheless, I wanted to see my artwork on public display—first at dawn, before Pender Street got crammed with parked cars, heavy traffic, and the so-called business of life. Later, the locale swarmed with shoppers forever and a day searching for sustenance. Finally, in the evening, the place was jammed with restaurant patrons fully intent on filling their bellies.

So I chose a number of strategic spots and looked in different ways. In one way, I could see how my creative efforts had no effect whatsoever on the larger scheme of things. Then again, if I flicked a switch in my mind, I could see how my pieces of coloured floral paper pasted on lampposts and telephone poles stood out.

Chinatown was my first choice in art galleries. It was an arcane place where I would eventually find my art in everything and everyone—in life, as I enthused about the thing to my friend and fellow artist Jim Wong-Chu, who happily seconded the notion. And, really, all I needed to do was stay hidden and quietly watch. Empty my mind of junk thoughts! My favourite pastime was being ghostlike anyway.

Jim Wong-Chu was a name that Jimmy chose for himself. He came at me with a story about being a paper son, so he had to choose between two surnames. Was I even listening with my half-baked brainpower? "Keep both," I cheerily sang out to him. In lots of free-spirited ways, I felt like I was the one to name him. Besides, it had a nice ring to it. And I had way more important issues to discuss with him.

I favoured a pastel image of Ivy Ling Po because she was an eternal favourite of my mother's generation. I insisted on a sly expression of youth and added some sappy blooms to her cheek. It's funny how a pretty face commands attention.

Some pedestrians looked harder than others. A few stopped to search for the message, but the printed notices I put up in Chinatown had no apparent purpose at all. So everyone turned away and continued on their way. And none of the flimsy newsprint fared well in the rainy Vancouver days that followed.

Simple in theory, harder in practice, more ebullient than well thought out, and with so much unspoken, my meaning, or want of, was at best a coy effort on my part. Or maybe I did it because I needed, as the cliché demanded, to find myself back then.

Decades later, I stared at Jimmy's shiny white forelock and he watched me squint like a nerd (because through thick or thin, no prescription for eyeglasses helped anymore), as we warned each other of hungry ghosts that continued to crazy-make everywhere. And spoke about the ways to resist such hyper-capitalistic devastation with all possible social-cultural-political twists.

I was impressed to hear that Jimmy's seminal book of poetry was banned by Chinatown in the past. But he didn't have to explain it to me. His simple take on being human, and the poetic act of forgiving oneself for being just so, started me on my self-dubbed way as a hunger artist. His book-cover photo of Mao defaced, unsparing and ethereal at the same time, has become for me an iconic inspiration.

Chinese people despise the notion of being *jian (diin* in Cantonese)—dismal, abject, defeated, and really lowdown. They also fear it brings terrible luck. As it was bluntly explained to me: better dead than *jian gui!* So I can see how Jimmy's little book of poems with its seemingly scanty message may have been cold-shouldered by his more image-happy fellow Chinese Canadians. But like him, I don't worry about his apparent lack of decorum.

Jim wasn't afraid of putting a voice to our darker, more vulnerable side. Thanks to that impulse, we can go that much further in broad daylight. We can forthrightly ask after the more global quandary of soul debt, because when we get right down to questions about the precious and precarious balance of life—who is human and who might be ghost? Or one better—where does the haunting part end and the human part begin? Ol' Jim would happily agree that we're all in this together.

SKY LEE

Hey, Jim

It's Paul, Paul Yee, shouting out from Toronto.

When I got over the shock about your latest news, I said to myself, "Jim, you've got to come back to us. People across the country, and around the world, are rooting for you. You're an indispensable part of many lives and communities, and you are much loved."

In the 1970s, when you and I first met, you had so many different circles of people that no one person really knew the "complete" you. This was part of your mystique, being worldly, having an artistic vision, and owning a multi-faceted skill set that surprised all your friends.

Back then, you were a few years older than me (you still are, and I want this situation to continue for a long, long time). I was still a student, and oh! how I envied you. You worked full time, you had a steady income, you drove a Datsun 240Z, and most importantly, you had freedom to do whatever you wanted.

Doesn't everyone yearn for independence?

You were an early pilgrim to San Francisco, where you met kindred souls in the arts and in community politics, people like Corky Lee, Nancy Hom, and Jim Dong. You sensed first-hand the rising energy and potential in the Asian communities of America. You brought back books, posters, artwork, music—to inspire us to look beyond our local horizons.

You were one of the few young people to have a "place" in Chinatown (though I often wondered how you found parking). Your studio at 15 East Pender, with its low ceiling and dark back rooms, let photography happen, let *Pender Guy* get started, and let people hang out somewhere safe and cool. You didn't live there, but you paid many years of rent, because your instinct said, "Jim, you need to be there."

You've always been a free thinker. Remember when you wouldn't buy a membership in the Chinese Cultural Centre, then the brash new player in town, because you wanted to be an outside observer who could keep criticizing it? Chinatown fought many issues over the Firehall, Barbecue Meats, the Green Paper on Immigration, etc., but you, you always chose your battles carefully. Didn't you go through a phase of reading and rereading Sunzi's *The Art of War*?

Wait, let me to go back to your circles of friends.

You were/are fluent in Cantonese, so you had Hong Kong friends: the Manson brothers, the many beautiful women whom I only saw in your black-and-white photographs, and the skinny kids who called you "sifu" because you taught them gung-fu. You always had the newest "fringe" magazines from Hong Kong about art and politics, because the discussions over there seemed far more advanced than our local situation.

Back then, as now, you have many artist friends, Alvin and Cecilia, Ron Yip, Ho Tung. I'd see your works framed and hung on walls at art exhibits. Most of us, we were volunteers, we were curious about Chinatown, but we sure weren't artists. You were one of the few artists that we knew. And your artistic vision drew people to you, young people who were curious about you and, in turn, who were encouraged by you, people like Helen Koyama, Barry Hong, Artson Seto.

You and I, we met in Chinatown. You wanted to run a "grass dragon" for the mid-autumn festival. People here knew nothing about it, but you were one of the few who had seen it in China, and you convinced a bunch

of people to help: to cut grass, weave a serpent-like body, build the dragon's head, and to light this magical beast with incense sticks and run it along Pender Street. That grass dragon has never been done again. It's one of my best and strongest memories of Chinatown.

Back then, we young people cultivated long shaggy hair and wore bell-bottom jeans and tie-dyed T-shirts. You designed several silkscreen logos for *Pender Guy*'s T-shirts, one of which featured the all-time hero Monkey King.

Here's the thing. You have a vision, you have a huge sense of community, and you've long been moving it along, on your own and with kindred souls.

You documented us with your photographs. You met tons of people in your daily swings through the markets and eateries of Chinatown. This was our "community," people from here and away, speaking only Chinese, only English, or maybe both. You saw these people often; they trusted you, shouted out greetings, made room for you, and let you take intimate photos of them at work.

Those images were honest and true: Chinatown was about people and work, history and belonging. In the faces of your subjects, you caught forever their hopes and dreams, and their life wisdoms, all of which were part of what it meant to be Chinese Canadian at that time.

You collected Chinatown. During one of many demolitions on Pender Street, you rescued two second-floor windows, old glass in ancient wooden frames, with two Chinese words painted boldly in gold to be seen from the street. The two words were "sieu heen." Translated, they meant "laughing corner," which was a private gambling club. My uncle was a member for decades, and he went there every day. That was his way of making a living.

You have an insatiable curiosity about making things better. When you discovered how yeast posed a danger to the human body, you told everyone, "Stop ingesting it!" When you learned about curcumin, you handed out pills and said, "You gotta try this. This will really help!" You found a talented masseuse newly arrived from China and dragged me to see her because of my sore shoulder. The treatment made me scream with pain. And now you're into brown rice and organics. So, tell me, why didn't you ever get into yoga, when you had Marlene right there for you?

Your eye was unparalleled in the photographs you took. That precious gift established the humanity and universality of the people and places you were drawn too. A single photo of yours was worth far more than "a thousand words."

But, then, you got into words. You pushed the envelope and broke out of the darkroom to go study poetry and write. You impressed the noted poet Michael Yates and published *Chinatown Ghosts* with Arsenal Pulp Press, our publisher in common.

Do you see that your art is travelling full circle, going from images to poetry, and then returning to pictures when your words sketch out rich, personal worlds in the minds of your readers?

The photos and words gathered in your portfolio "Pender Street East" were spectacular. It's a collector's item, and I'm glad it's safe in the archives.

You care about history, and you care about stories. You and *Pender Guy Radio* went out to document the stories of the Chinese on Vancouver Island, as well as the record of Chinese Canadian veterans of the Second World War.

You recognize the power of words. Stories need to be published to reach audiences, so you pushed the anthologies of Chinese Canadian writing, the Asian Canadian Writers' Workshop, *Ricepaper Magazine,* and the annual LiterASIAN conferences.

You know everyone in the literary community, but you also have a keen eye for writing. Remember when you read my early outline for *A Superior Man*? You saw that my ending didn't work and told me so, early on, so I changed it and saved myself much embarrassment.

Mohamed says hi and recalls how you and Marlene stayed with us in August 2003 during the great power outage in Toronto. For once, it was dark enough for people to lie on the grass and gaze up at the stars. Then, at dinner with Dora Nipp, we talked and laughed and there wasn't a moment of silence.

Jim, you and I didn't always agree; we've had long, loud arguments at meetings and over the phone. There were times when I couldn't understand you, you didn't understand me, and we had to agree to disagree because of our different communication styles. But we stayed friends because we're moving forward in an unstoppable movement that is way bigger than both of us put together.

Jim, you started many things, and there's much more yet to be done, so come on back to us. Soon.

PAUL YEE

BE SPECIFIC (LIKE PACIFIC OCEAN)

you specify—I'll modify

declassify

amplify

rectify

the menu

Jim Wong-Chu has changed the lives of so many,

connecting us to our histories, to each other, to a feeling of being part
of a larger cultural movement. He showed his dedication to community
through his writing, editorial work, and organizing of the Asian Canadian
Writers' Workshop (ACWW). The ACWW is one of the reasons why I
moved from Calgary to Vancouver in the 1990s. I felt the pull and the
need for writers of Asian descent to come together *against* the racist
systems that have sought to exploit, restrict, and define us, and *for* the
much longer history, present, and future that is rightfully ours.

In my early years in Vancouver, I remember visiting Jim at his place
on 41st, listening to stories, talking about everything from dong quai
(ways to make that strengthening herbal broth near your moon time)
to *Inalienable Rice* and *Pender Guy Radio*. He was a calm, steadfast rock,
who encouraged so many of us. It was always reassuring to know that he
was there. And his spirit continues to guide us, I believe.

Chinatown Ghosts faces the haunted house known as Canada with
open eyes. Jim's poem "equal opportunity" even-handedly and humor-
ously mocks the racism that is historically blatant and that remains to
be overcome today in its new forms. In the face of colonial attempts to

divide and control, life and grace intervene from the bottom up. His poems recognize the scripts and expectations that have been imposed on us, finding moments of humour in the refusals to perform on cue, the range of asiancy that permeates our everyday world. From the newspaper vending *kwan yin* to the "chinese workers / pitching girders / sometimes / solitary/ sometimes / blood spattered / sweating / and singing / while the moon shines / a spotlight / on them," the poems honour working-class people's lives with brevity and compassion, pragmatism and love. They also quietly reach beyond the human realm to address rain and monsoon, buddha and the disappearing moon.

I benefited a lot from the work of the ACWW to overcome systemic racism in the publishing industry. It was an honour to receive the first Emerging Writers Award from the ACWW for my manuscript *monkey-puzzle*. Jim helped me navigate that time, and I'll always be grateful to him and to the ACWW for their dedication to Asian Canadian cultures, which are grounded in a dedication to social justice and decolonization, because we understand that "until all of us have made it, none of us have made it," as Rosemary Brown said. Although I wasn't around for the times when Jim, SKY Lee, Lee Maracle, and other writers hung out together on the unceded Coast Salish territories also known as Vancouver, I cherish the legacy and the stories they pass on to us.

RITA WONG

Jim. Beautiful Jim. Wherever you are, this is your book.

Not ours. You have spent countless hours uplifting our words, and now it's our job to read yours.

Silently stepping aside in wonder and awe of you,

CATHERINE HERNANDEZ

I picked up Jim's book *Chinatown Ghosts* in 1986. The cover was at once beautiful and ominous. The shredded Mao Zedong poster on a Chinatown lamppost (in Vancouver, I assumed) was compelling and perhaps emblematic of Jim's life—a paper son coming to a new land and tearing up memories of his homeland. It was ominous because of its lack of promise, its foretelling of a life of struggle.

Yet the poetry within the book's pages spoke of hope. His luminous and unique imagery and Asian Canadian sensibilities spoke of a distinctly Asian poet fighting for a place in the Canadian literary landscape.

Jim rose above all the struggles to become a leading visionary for Asian Canadian writing. I remember talking with him about his projects: the Asian Canadian Writers' Workshop, the Go for Broke Revue, the Asian Heritage Month festivities, *Ricepaper Magazine,* the LiterASIAN writers festival, and a host of other events. Throughout them all, he was consistent in his ambition to raise the profiles of Asian Canadian art and artists. He never wavered or compromised in his vision, and he never flagged in enthusiasm and energy.

In return, I never turned him down when he invited me to appear on stage or in the pages of the above. I did so because he never let me down whenever I needed his help. He always had time for me.

For his efforts, he was recognized with the Queen's Diamond Jubilee Medal, the Queen's Golden Jubilee Medal, and the Human Rights Media Award of B'nai Brith Canada, to name a few.

But Jim was much more than his awards and projects. Recently, I took *Chinatown Ghosts* from my bookshelf and turned to the title page. He had signed my copy with "Thanks Terry, we've got to get you published!"

That was Jim, always encouraging Asian Canadian writers to write. And he backed that encouragement by giving advice and representing AC writers to publishers. As I said, he never let me down.

For some reason, I fancifully passed my index finger over his writing and felt the indentation of his pen in the paper. And there he was; miraculously, Jim came back to me. I could see him sitting calmly at performances and readings, quietly dispensing advice to would-be writers, scattering words of wisdom at a conference, or holding court before a gathering of friends at some Chinese restaurant. I smiled in those warm memories. Then he faded sadly with my thoughts of his passing. I felt the loss deeply and profoundly. But I then realized he will always be there for me and others, maybe not in body but in spirit ... like one of his fabled Chinatown ghosts.

TERRY WATADA

at the end of my life

will I too have walked a full circle

and arrive like you

an old elephant

to his grave?

These lines from the end of Jim's poem "fourth uncle"

remind me how immersed Jim was in the circle of life, and death. He always had his eye on the "full circle" of his world, from an epic awareness of Chinese history and mythology, a comprehensive view of his community and its possibilities to be creative, to how to sustain one's health properly. One of his last gestures towards my own bodily quirks was to share with me a small vial of pure turpentine, "to be taken ..." etc. And when I first met him in the '80s he advised me of my "real" Chinese name and ancestry.

What I meant when I wrote on the original dust jacket "The cadences of these poems are photographic" is that their poetic sensibility is rooted in an amazing capacity to envision. Jim translated his photographic skill into a poetic and lyric aperture that is constantly open to the music of language; these are poems where the eye becomes the ear. The careful attention to the intricacy of sound in lines like "amos falls / off his elbow" is a compositional awareness not only of a picture of the stripper dancing at the Kubla Khan nightclub but of a rhythmic cadence that fits the mood of the moment.

I see the poems of *Chinatown Ghosts* not just as snapshots of a time and place gone by but as a necessary and panoramic part of Jim's struggle to envision a world that acknowledges difference. He parlayed his creativity, as we know, into a wide range of public presences that have helped establish a pre-eminent body of Asian Canadian writing and provide a space for new writing. These poems are a testament to the power of art to walk the "full circle," like "an old elephant"—gently, with strength, patience, and intelligence.

FRED WAH

We'come a Chinatowng, Folks! Ha. Ha. Ha ... Happy New Year! Fred Eng, "Freddie" of Eng's Chinatown tour'n'travoo.

"We tell Chinatown where to go." Ha ha ha. I'm top guide here. Allaw week Chinee New Year. Ssssshhh Boom! Muchee Muchie firey crackee! Ha. Ha. Ha ...

But you're my last tour of the day, folks. And on my last tour of the day, no hooey. I like to let my hair down. Drop the phony accent. And be me. Just me.

I figure once a day, I have got to be me.

—from *The Year of the Dragon,* by Frank Chin

tradition

I grasp
in my hand
a bundle of rice
wrapped in leaves
forming triangles

I pull the string
unlocking the tiny knot
releasing the long strand
which binds

I tug at the dry green leaves
holding the sweet rice within

peeling it back
I begin to open

how feel I do?

your eyes plead approval
on each uttered word

and even my warmest smile
cannot dispel the shamed muscles
from your face

let me be honest
with you

to tell the truth
I feel very much at home
in your embarrassment

don't be afraid

like you
I was mired in another language
And I gladly surrendered it
for english

you too
in time
will lose your mother's tongue

and speak
at least as fluent
as me

now tell me

how do you feel?

baptism 1909

god
an easier word than
christian ... kisjin

his tongue grinds
like dry bread
bumping against each syllable

k-k-kkkrrrrrrrrrrrrrr

missus murray
reverend murray's wife
corrects him
for the ninth time

krrrrrriiiisttttiiiiaaannnnn

he stares
at this woman giant
then
timidly
offers her an O

koooooooooisjin

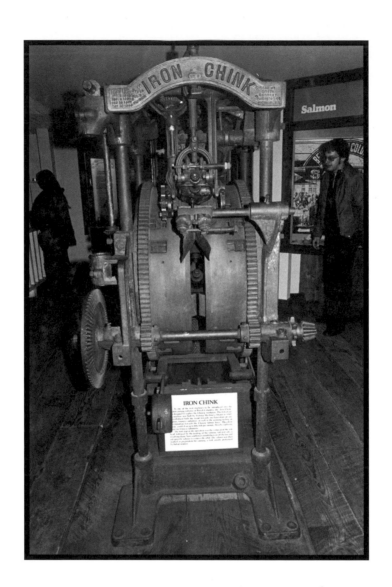

equal opportunity

in early canada
when railways were highways

each stop brought new opportunities

there was a rule

> the chinese could only ride
> the last two cars
> of the trains

that is

until a train derailed
killing all those
in front

(the chinese erected an altar and thanked buddha)

a new rule was made

> the chinese must ride
> the front two cars
> of the trains

that is

until another accident
claimed everyone
in the back

(the chinese erected an altar and thanked buddha)

after much debate
common sense prevailed

the chinese are now allowed
to sit anywhere
on any train

mother

she always wears her silence
in front of father

funny tho

none of us
brothers or sisters
ever woke
when they made love
and that must have been often
because there are many of us
and some knew they were not wanted

those were the days
before birth control pills
and condoms
at least the cheap ones

we were poor

funny tho

father never gave her money
to buy food
preferring to buy it himself
but she fed us
I never understood this

in the morning
she'd be up before us
fixing our breakfast *jook*
and after packing us off to school
she'd start her wash
by hand

---

jook: congee, rice porridge

cold soap water
wooden wash board
hand wrung
headless forms hung on bamboo poles
skewered shirtsleeves like flags
rows of crucifixes
baking in the dry wind

the day is long
with many goodbyes and hellos
before the night

while we sleep
in our one-room home

she mends the last of tomorrow's shirts
and quietly waits

for father

ice

was the first time
anyone remembers it happening

the fields froze
in our village
in south china

we broke some
not knowing what it was
and took it to the junk peddler

he thought it was glass
and traded us a penny
for it

he wrapped it up
in old cloth and placed it
on top of his basket

of course
the noon day sun melted it

by the time
we came back with more
he had gotten wise

fourth uncle

we met in Victoria

we talked and discovered
our similar origins

you a village relative
while I a young boy
sitting quietly on the other side
of the coffee table
cups between us

we are together
for the moment
but I feel far from you

you said
you travelled and worked
up and down this land
and now you have returned
to die

to be buried
beside the others
in the old chinese cemetery
by the harbour
facing the open sea
facing home

at the end of my life
will I too have walked a full circle

and arrive like you
an old elephant
to his grave?

journey to merritt

this is the last train

ever

next week I must leave by greyhound
not to say I care
the CPR is not my father

tracks clicked as I watch
the disappearing moon

flashing

as signals do
before a change of rails

the cold breeze whips by

and every mile
I see chinese workers

pitching girders

sometimes
solitary

sometimes
blood spattered

sweating
and singing

while the moon shines
a spotlight

on them

old chinese cemetery   kamloops   july 1977

like a child lost
wandering about
touching   feeling
tattered grounds
touching   seeing
wooden boards

etched in ink
etched in weather
etched in fading memories
etched
faded
forgotten

I walk
on earth
above the bones
of a multitude
of golden mountain men
searching for scraps
of memory

like a child unloved
his face pressed hard
against the wet window

peering in
for a desperate moment
I touch my past

the oldest

her teeth died

was it before her husband
or after her last children?

the newspaper vending *kwan yin*

1
she got her bedroom eyes
from
selling papers

in front of yen fong's
at
eight below

her bloodless face
unpainted
cracks
at the break of dawn

2
your every turn brings you closer
to her

busy street

the surge forces the air
into
a thinning corridor

her hand outstretched
before you

3
you tempt her
with
a large bill

(she loves forgotten money)

––––––––––––

kwan-yin: Goddess of mercy

so
naturally
she short-changes you

(surtax on the careless)

4
you catch her
but
before you can act

she swallows your tongue

your mind raging
in the wind

5
In a world
of
unrepentant sinners

buddhas
must survive

there is no malice in this game

she is not
your lover
and
owes you nothing

you will understand

when you see her
at
the end of day

dragging her shadow
softly
through the rain

scenes from the mon sheong home for the aged
(for li wang-fai)

1
she spends her waking hours
counting every item

something is always missing

she insists
there are ghosts
lurking behind her in the shadows

snapping up a thing or two
when she turns her head

a rope she wove with strings
she collected ties her bedpost
to her alarm clock in impossible knots

on every outing she brings home
new locks and chains

they lace her room
like snakes

her tongue
her only defense

she spits everywhere
hoping to catch one
and pin it helpless
against the wall
for everyone to see
to prove she meant
business

2
their love is souring
again

in desperation
she pulls his hands
towards her long dried breasts
tucked firm with bra
and tissue

she hopes
that he won't go again
to the night duty nurse
(the pretty one)
to ask for another transfer
from the ward

he does

but this time
the young nurse only listens politely
and promises to talk to the director
in the morning

she is wise not to interfere
with the lovers

the scratch on her forehead
a reminder

3
he had walked this coast
and ate chinook when he had to

his eyes sparkle on talk

this was a fuller page
of his life

he remembers the road building accident
in 1910

his body among the rubble
blood of dead men ran
thick as pig
so thick
he had to lift his head
to breathe

the *gwai low* engineer
gave wrong instruction
with the dynamite

"I lucky"

the break in his leg
did not pop the skin

"bing sum saved me
he, a good bone setter"

but he was laid up for a year
on other days
his mind draws blanks
and circles

"too many knocks on the noggin
too much bad blood inside"

———————

gwai low: white demon (black english: motherfucker)

he spent the next day
staring at a wall in the lobby

turning only once to ask

"where is my china?"

someone laughed and told him
it was directly below his feet
on the other side of the world

in the morning
a nurse found him
at the union station
dressed in his going-out clothes
his suitcase at his side
clutching tickets for home

listen listen

I am captured

a willing victim

the old man speaks
time stands still
very still

I hear the PAK PAK
of his heartbeat
trapped between words
uttered in panic
hurrying
afraid the thin thread between us
would slacken
break loose

forever

it's all right
I will listen
listen to all

but
his reminiscence
of sixteen-hour workdays
has no time for time

the old country
(for tony hoy)

she gave me three letters

her daughter's son
wants to marry
send a thousand

a sister's nephew
has a first-born
send three hundred

her stepson
in hong kong
gambled his wages
anything will do

aunt ling has a pension
and no savings

she asked me
to help her
divide ten dollars
and send each an equal share

jimmy the waiter

I caught him picking his nose
and flicking the snot
into the cream of mushroom soup

(that's for calling me chink)

I know him and he wouldn't
hurt a fly

but would think nothing
of serving it up
with crackers

hippo luck
(for sid tan)

carmen smiles
hand in hand
we glide the flamenco air

the dance floor whirled a common dish
we danced a pair of common fish

stewing in the back room heat
where men grow thinner
than gambler's chips

I am a miner of the mountain of gambler's gold
between bowls of borrowed rice
I toss the dice of low life

numb to the feel of each burning tile
its clatter a swirling tatter of dancing steps

stay with me ... carmen ...
as surely as lord buddha sits on my right
make it all or nothing
tonight

the egg roll kid

nimble fingers
working the thin moist
egg roll skin

sizzling grease
the colour of hide

he hums a lively tune

the fractured music
breaking my brain

I feel his nothing

his no hope

the no going home

because home and his young wife

are in deep fried
vietnam

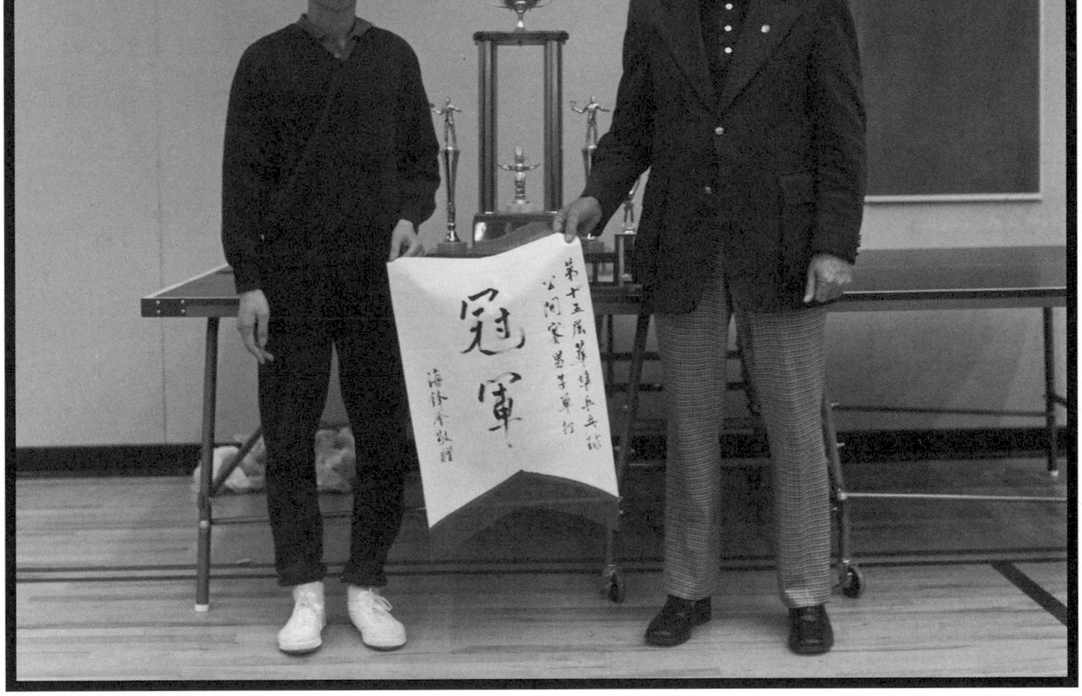
Chinatown Open Table Tennis Championships
3
冠軍

the gospel according to edsel ford fung

(a found poem)

NO BS
NO JIVING
NO MISTAKES

ALL FOODS—NO BOOZE—NO COFFEE
NO FORTUNE COOKIES—NO SOFT DRINKS

<u>CHECK IT OUT</u>—<u>ONE BY ONE</u>

a bowl of soup is like a whole meal

<u>BE PRECISE AND CONCISE ON EVERY LITTLE THING</u>

say what kind of vegetables

chow fun is big flat wide noodles like
pasta—with meat and chinese greens or
bean sprouts

<u>BE SPECIFIC (LIKE PACIFIC OCEAN)</u>

chow mein is pan fried lo mein soft
noodles—with beef pork chinese
green shrimp chicken sprouts
etc.

sweet & sour pork can be rice plate
or chow mein—or just meat (three
ways)

<u>BE VERY PRECISE ABOUT IT</u>

chow yuk could be chinese greens or bean
sprouts with roast pork or beef shrimp
or chicken could be meat only rice

plate or with soft noodles—skinny or
flat

fried shrimp is an appetizer—actually
it is a ripoff—expensive but not
filling

check the middle section of the menu

BE PRECISE ON EVERY LITTLE THING

your way or my way—
I'll bring—you eat
      or
you name—I'll get

DON'T LEAVE ANYTHING OUT

you write—I'll rewrite
you specify—I'll modify
      declassify
       amplify
        rectify

       the menu

centipede

here here they come dressed
in blues smart the first day iron
a mild sky blue uniformed parade blue
flurry of tiny fists and red scarfs
winding down bannister staircase swinging
swinging out to open space where sudden frenzy
shatters reflection

it appears again in the horizon long after
you thought it gone for forever this time
a red star etched in its forehead
red crimson gold golden metallic gait
swinging left right right left
shouting together loud this time
in rank confusion

of course there are ghosts

my aunt remembers
as a young girl
sitting
by the sun-lit window
watching the warm dust
dance

always
in the darkest corner
a figure
having no legs or waist
would appear

he is here again
she said to herself

and why not?

he probably deserves
to be here
as much as I

what fun it be
she said to me
to be able to come and go
like so many
half memories

herself nodding
to sleep

coffee ghosts

if the coffee in your cup is gone
without an explanation

check for its traces
in the bottom of the mug

feel not vexed nor the least hexed
by this unwarranted intrusion

pay up your fifty cents
consider it well spent

in chinatown, the tastiest of drinks
is harder to resist than you think

the south china homecoming of klondike lee

you hold your firstborn
for the first time

he sniffles
his blotchy red buddha nose
his tiny face blown like a balloon

the proud grandmother says
he looks just like you

you laugh

your laughter greets the quiet eyes
of your wife

she coughs

making you tuck the folds
of warm blankets closer around her neck

soon they will all be faded images
on a photograph

drawn in solitude

until the edges break
and fall
like snow flakes
onto the frozen caribou tundra

it is winter in your village
and for the first time in ten years
you will miss snow

pender street east

fresh rock cod
a pleasant smile
roast pork fresh hot
taste before you buy
(guarantee to satisfy)
ginger green onions
soy sauce   msg

take a break
across the street
find a booth
order green tea
relax ...
where else would you possibly
want to be?

curtain of rain
(from paul yee)

curtain of rain
another act unfolds

chinatown
forever changing
you and I
actors audience
watching being watched

pender street east
nothing dampens its spirit

quiet yet dignified
unassuming yet proud
hidden under umbrellas
steady as raindrops

old friend

screaming sirens pull me closer

I hit
the wall of backs
looking for a crack
to squeeze through

clawing
between the rooted feet
to get to you
because your voice
keeps mumbling my name

where is your pain?

our nightly talk
of green hills
the cool breeze and your village
mocks these tenement walls

you told me
you were sick only once before

your frail body was carried
by members of your family
on a bamboo stretcher
along the rice fields
to the well
it was you mother's name
you called then

she cradled you
onto her back
and tucked you in
like a kitten

her warm hands reaching
down her shoulder

to touch your neck

inspection of a house paid in full

I could not hide
my curiosity at your pride
in paying cash in full

perhaps it was
because you arrived
in canada
young and penniless

while working at our restaurant
you came up with the strangest notion
that some day
when you own your own place
you could get away
with substituting ink
for coffee

(cheap profitable imitation)

those wild hopeful impossibilities
made yours a rocky one man road
up the golden mountain

yet you made it

and today
looking me squarely in the eye
you tell me you have arrived
your family at your side

my last words
are

BEWARE THE TAXMAN

tickles

pretty anna
a sweet fourteen
flutters in and out
of the party
detonating armpits

spiriting her cache out the back
a flock of friends in tow
she riots the stolen laughter
into the waiting air

meanwhile
inside the house
uncle bing
the family clown
begs laughter by balancing
ice cubes from his rum and coke
on his red nose

as she enters
their eyes exchange chuckles
not missing a beat
she cruises on
her terrorist fingers seeking

seagull afternoon

feet moving in tandem
weave like roving timid eyes
around the thick chinatown saturday

one brave bird
half-steps towards
the curb

its next step
a bottomless eternity

elbows raised
in flight

at the cue of green light

it trots out
an unflustered two-step

peasants

my father came
from the rice fields
to the city
and there he stayed

just yesterday
I sat and wondered
about all this

what does it mean

rice fields
a glittering city
I try to touch

both ends
are perhaps
a bridge
a causeway
linking rainbows
sunny wet afternoons

from green rice fields
to glittering city
the green and glitter merge

steadily quietly

outside my window
it is raining

today the rain

nourishes rice fields
nourishes the city
nourish me

boundary bay

(for robert kikuchi-yngojo and rick shiomi)

sitting on the edge
one side we see
the other side
the horizon

robert draws faces
on beach rocks
while we talk
about things past
things to come

the sun burns us
we don't care

there's the border

eating fish

closing in
like a whiff of death

these february blues rollick
up the kinks of my spine
stumbling over each knot

where are you elvis chong when I need you?

we used to drag our roots
down the chonk-stepping chinatown
for *char siu bao*

singing for dinners
into the night
like two cats in the rain

shit

I wish I could chuck my head
into the wastebasket
and moon walk
over the easy chair

---

char siu bao: barbeque pork bun

memories of old kubla khan nightclub

WWWOWWWWW TURN ME ON

heads rolling sideways to catch
a better glimpse
of miss choo choo la chong

her bashful body curling up
the papermaché-wrapped staircase
our corkscrewing necks reaching
for air

STRUT YER STUFF BABY

I'M SO HIGH I KIN FOLLA YA TA HEAVEN

she glides down the firepole
and whips open her thighs

amos falls
off his elbow

we

a bunch of junior chinatown cowboys
center stage
surrounded by a bunch of oldtimers
eating peanuts

with no teeth

and poor old fast eddie's face
a little grey

'cause
he no go pee
until the break

BREAK MAN

GIVE THE POOR MAN A BREAK

YIIIIIPPPPPEEEEEEEEEEEEEEEEE

JUNIOR CHINATOWN COWBOYS RIDE AGAIN

dreams

as you make
your final turn
passing through
the dividing doors arriving
at the threshold
between that which is discernable
and that which is not

you will find me there
waiting
ready to catch you
as you fall

nearing

here we are
parting once more
but there is no sadness

such is the way
with old friends

you have not changed
I have not changed
you pick through my hair
and discover whiteness
while I stare at
an increasing forehead

monsoon

I crawled
under the table
covered by thick blankets
to feel your warm caress
smell the tropical steam
you gave off
as you hit the pavement

the aerialist

are you the pilot
are you really the pilot
are you in control
I want a parachute

the world outside is cold
and crappy
and I can't stand the wind

I can't swim

can you understand
do you know what I'm saying
am I coming in clear
I am a spy

I see trees
I see branches
I see leaves
I see you breathing on me

not the first time

we have our own ways
of mistreating ourselves

lost time is hard
to retrieve

you said
time solves all

in an effort
to understand

I forgot

rain

it seems so long ago

I remember seeing you coming
from beyond the open sea

you brushed the sun-green mountains
grey
while I sat on the rooftop
with friends
laughing
waiting for you

do you still remember
that time
I challenged you to a race
to my doorstep
and won?

medley in ink and brush

studio landing

one stroke of sun descends
in fluid swirling brilliance

we bond ourselves
like bamboo brush and cuttle ink
to the soft rice paper

diffused
translucent
whole

bodies emerge
singular

ourselves each defined

merritt b.c. revisited 1965

1
catch a look at
them mainstreetin' wildflowers

HOOOooooo SHE'S SO FINE
cruising down
the one-street-main-drag-town
hooting away

me and the Yano brothers
three asians
in a '57 ford-niagra-
not-so-flashy-model-blue

but we struck out
like the morning sun

2
the canada cafe's
THE PLACE
no other

delicious waitresses
pushing
hamburgers
fries
fried rice on the grill

we three
devour the mix
like demons

laughing
chasing rice pudding

out the door

3

coldwater river
precarious lifeline

our poles over the side
half pound test
(no lures)

save a gentle
persuasive
occasional tug

enough is
always not enough

starlings plow
the vacant sky

JIM WONG-CHU was born in Hong Kong in 1949 and came to Canada in 1953. He was a poet, author, editor, and historian, and co-founded the Asian Canadian Writers' Workshop, *Ricepaper Magazine*, the *Pender Guy Radio* program, the Asia Canadian Performing Arts Resource (ACPAR), LiterASIAN: A Festival of Asian Canadian Writing, and Vancouver Asian Heritage Month. The first edition of *Chinatown Ghosts*, released in 1986, was one of the first poetry books ever published by a Chinese Canadian poet. Jim was the co-editor of *Many-Mouthed Birds: Contemporary Writing by Chinese Canadians*, co-edited by Bennett Lee (Douglas & McIntyre), *Swallowing Clouds: An Anthology of Chinese-Canadian Poetry*, co-edited by Andy Quan (Arsenal Pulp Press), and *AlliterAsian: Twenty Years of Ricepaper Magazine*, co-edited by Allan Cho and Julia Lin (Arsenal Pulp Press). Jim is perhaps best known for his unwavering support of Asian Canadian writers, many of whom have gone on to achieve international success. He was also a full-time letter carrier for Canada Post for thirty years. Jim Wong-Chu passed away in 2017.